I0522426

THE INSIDE WORLD
In Memory of W.H. Auden

POEMS

William Clarence Graham

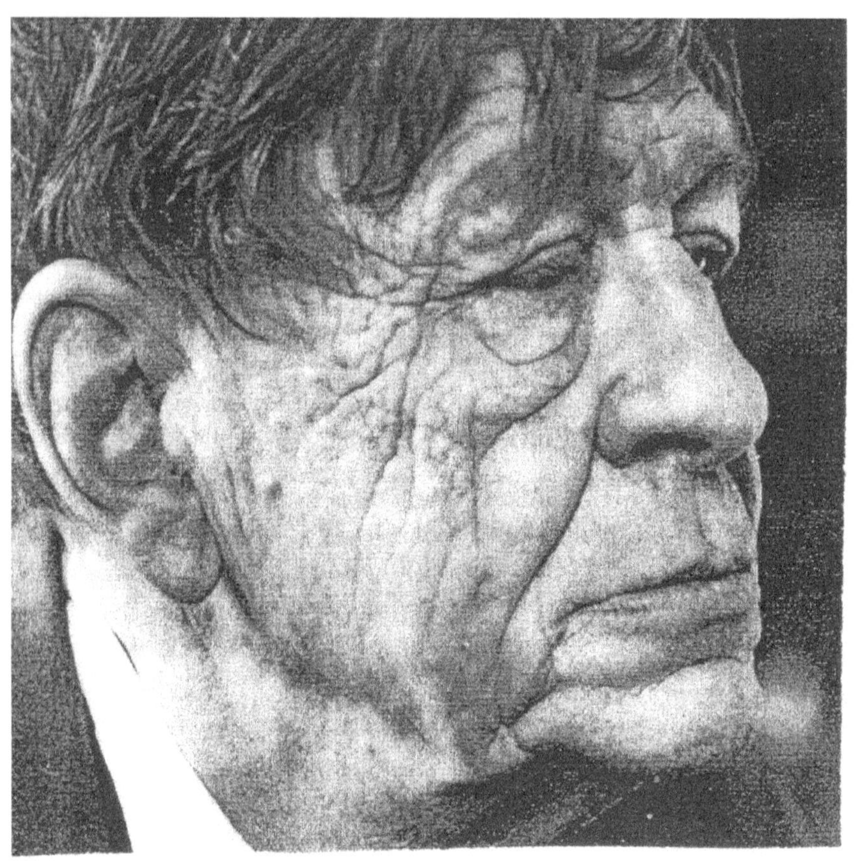

Auden was notoriously messy,

But never vain.

He was humourous and funny,

And said of his face,

"It looks like a wedding cake

Left out in the rain."

DEDICATION

This set of poems is intended to commemorate the 50th anniversary of the death of Wystan Hugh Auden, who died on 29 September, 1973.

Auden was the foremost English language poet of the 20th century. He was hailed as the greatest anti-war poet of his age. Critics (such as Edward Mendelson, Kieran Andrieu, Oliver Teale, etc.) praise his 'radical, defiant humanism' driven by a deep-seated concern for racism, genocide and injustice much of it inspired by fascism. Some of his contemporaries – Ezra Pound and Gertrude Stein – had even flirted with fascist ideals while Auden himself joined the Spanish Civil War against fascism. In life, as well as in his work, he was politically engaged. He despised the authoritarian power of strong men and tyrants. He would have opposed today's examples of Putin and Trump. He disapproved also of the school of Modernist authors (T.S. Eliot and others) whose aesthetic mistakenly thought of the past as grand and theoretically organic in relation to the present age. Auden did not idealize the past ("History is a squalid mess") or have any doubts about the necessary struggles of living in the present age ("Leap before you Look"). He was a man of the present in which he lived. To the very end of his life he concentrated on the sufferings and oppression of his fellow citizens. He believed in the collaborative goal of human solidarity.

As a student of literature, and from the time that I began writing poetry, I adopted Auden as my poetic mentor. Later, I questioned his assertion that "Poetry makes nothing happen." It happens in us, I said. I described poetry as "the alchemy of the Inside World' – that is, to distinguish poetry from science, history, and religion; (and I described philosophy as 'the medicine of the Inside World'). Alchemy, the ancients said, was the art or practice of transmuting everyday basic materials into rich and valuable things (*e.g.*, from lead into gold). That is what poetry does.

Thanks to Peter H. Salus, my friend and colleague (and Professor of Linguistics) at the University of Toronto (Scarborough), it was my great privilege to spend some time with Wystan Auden himself in person on several occasions in Canada and Austria. They are among my most treasured memories. (See my poem "Auden's Slippers" below.) He had come to Toronto to work on the Norse Poetic Edda. In the Spring of 1972, a little more than a year before Auden's death, Peter and I travelled to Wystan's home in Kirchstetten, Austria, at his invitation, for a visit. There we met Auden's companion, fellow poet and librettist, Chester Kallman. We all went into town to get groceries that Chester needed for food. While Chester cooked, Auden read some late poems; and during dinner he played his phonograph.

I hope that these poems of a philosopher-poet, who has tried to follow, though inadequately, in Auden's footsteps, express some of the concerns of Auden himself about the human condition: suffering and oppression, and the responsibility of poets in the current age; his personal honesty and humility; and his ideal of a shared, collaborative, and caring humanity which Auden cites as "an affirming flame".

William Clarence Graham

A PROFESSIONAL COMMENT

William Graham's poems do more than pay tribute to W.H. Auden: they carry forward the spirit of Auden's poems in their own vivid, technically adept, and emotionally satisfying address to the reader. They speak eloquently and convincingly in the way that Auden always tried to do in his own work.

Very grateful for that superb essay on Auden. It deserves wide circulation. I think you've captured many things about him that are worth saying (see 'W.H. Auden – The Poet of Democratic Citizenship' on pp. 63 – 66).

Edward Mendelson,
Editor and Literary Executor of the Estate of W.H. Auden

IN GRATITUDE

I want to thank my wife, Mary McKechnie-Graham, for her full support and collaboration in preparing *The Inside World* book of poems I have intended to commemorate and celebrate the 50th anniversary of the 1973 death of poet W. H. Auden, the foremost English language poet of the 20th. century. I am grateful to her for her constant care. I began writing poetry in the 1950s as an MA graduate student in English Literature in California. (I am still not able to stop writing poetry any more than I can stop breathing.) Early on, I fell under the spell of the marvellously skillful work and word selection of Auden, and I considered him as my mentor to whom I was very grateful. I was even more grateful when he later became my friend.

I am grateful to the Hon. Bob Rae, Canada's Ambassador to the United Nations, whom I assisted, at his request, when he was suddenly elected Premier of Ontario (1990 – 1995) and I was honoured to provide some advice to his new government and his Minister of Colleges and Universities (see *About the Author*).

I am grateful also to my teachers and professors; to my students and colleagues at the University of Toronto and to all of my friends and family. Many of them had read some earlier versions of these poems in local school and university journals, and they often urged me to publish them wider. Working on my PhD in Philosophy and embarking on a Professorship there, however, caused me to set those pleas aside: that is, until I had the good fortune of being further encouraged by Professor Edward Mendelson of Columbia University who, knowing of my interest in Auden, asked to read some of my poems. Edward Mendelson is an Auden expert, and the Editor of many books on Auden; and he is also the Literary Executor of the Estate of W. H. Auden. His wonderfully encouraging words and review convinced me to embark on this venture.

I express my deepest gratitude to Antonia Pop, Vice-President of the University of Toronto Press, and her staff, including Sandra Shaw, Ashley Bernicky and Editor Suzanne Rancourt, for their extraordinary patience and understanding in reviewing my book, and their insight into what I have in mind, and especially for their very thoughtful decision to publish it.

I am grateful also to Catriona Kaufman of Top Kat Services who has skillfully edited and formatted much of my publishing activity, including the book *The Inside World*, and to Alan Kaufman for book layout and cover design.

I am grateful to all who love the poetry of W.H. Auden. He is the central character in this book, and to whose memory it is dedicated. Finally, I am grateful to anyone who chooses to read and enjoy my poems and essay in his honour. I would appreciate your comments. Thank you,

William Clarence Graham

IF YOU READ THIS BOOK

The Inside World contains some of my original poetry. I began writing poetry in earnest in the 1950s as a graduate student in English Literature at Loyola University (M.A. 1958). And I have continued writing poetry to this day. It has become as endemic as breathing. I chose the poems in this book to pay a tribute to one of the greatest poets of the recent past – Wystan Hugh Auden – in honour of the 50th anniversary of his sudden death in 1973. As a young student of poetry, I had adopted Auden as my mentor because his interests, themes and attitudes in poetry matched my own.

We were both interested in the complex, and sometimes contradictory, relationships between human persons; in love and suffering and death; in fascism and totalitarianism; and the remarkable resilience of which people are capable.

I was overjoyed when I learned that Auden had come to Toronto, Canada to work on the Nordic 'Poetic Edda' with Peter Salus, a Professor of Linguistics at the recently built University of Toronto College at Scarborough (later referred to as UTSC), the newest member of the family of colleges and institutes at University of Toronto. Salus was an expert on the ancient text, and Auden thought it contained a mention of a form of his family name. I had joined the University of Toronto in 1966, a year after its founding in 1965, as the first full-time philosopher at UTSC. Peter Salus was one of my closest friends and colleagues. I was delighted to be able to meet with Auden in person.

The Inside World is also a report on W.H. Auden's poetic work during his trip to Toronto, Canada. I was very grateful that he accepted my invitation to meet with my students at UTSC, to read and discuss some of his poetry with them, and to answer their questions. His enthusiasm showed how interested and excited he was to comply. His reading of his poetry at the University of Toronto (specifically at UTSC) is now a significant event in the history of poetry in Canada. My poem, "Auden's Slippers" in this book, was written while he was in Toronto and is based on his meeting with my students and my family. When it came time to eat, Auden wanted to experience Chinese Dim Sum, which was prevalent in the many Toronto Chinese restaurants but absent in his home town of Kirchstetten, Austria. He insisted that Peter and I should bring our entire families with him, and he delighted especially in spending time with the children like a surrogate grandfather. My children still remember his loving concern for them.

Auden was one of the most personable and generous people I have ever met. When he learned of my interest in poetry too, he treated me like a colleague and personal friend and wanted to see some of my work. I gave him copies of some of the poems in this book. When he met with my students, I was very surprised to hear that, along with reading his own work, he decided to discuss two of my poems. The poems he chose were "The Crime of Journalist Wallraff" and "At Dusk." During our wonderful discussions about poetry, he had learned that I was a professional philosopher with a love of poetry, and "At Dusk" deals, in part, with the relationship between poetry and philosophy. His own poetry, in my estimation, also shows us that, as a professional poet, he had a deep interest in philosophy too.

The Inside World also contains a poem written on the special occasion when I was called up for tenure as a Professor of Philosophy at the University of Toronto in 1976. The Committee wanted to examine my output and publications in philosophy, which was usual in my circumstances; but, having heard that I wrote poetry as well, they asked to see some of my poetry too. I sent them some examples but decided that I should write a special poem in honour of the Committee too. I wrote the mock-heroic poem – "Heracles to His Tenure Committee," included in the book. The last poem in the book is "Wystan Hugh Auden – In

Memoriam," written at the time of his death in 1973. It is a kind of echo of his own poem at the death of W.B. Yeats.

The Inside World also contains an essay that I wrote 50 years after his death to illustrate my strong belief that W.H. Auden's reputation had not only survived, but it had gained in the meantime, and that he must be considered a "poet of the ages," not simply a poet of the recent past – a poet and a philosopher as well. It is "W.H. Auden – The Poet of Democratic Citizenship." I hope that you will enjoy and agree with it.

Finally, *The Inside World* provides some details of my life ("About the Author"). It includes some of my important cases in dispute resolution which I studied at Harvard Law School and practiced at UTFA, OCUFA and the CAUT. They are as significant to me as my love and practice of poetry and philosophy. It reports on my efforts to save the academic career of the renowned hematologist, Dr. Nancy Olivieri, now Professor of Medicine at the University of Toronto, when she was unjustly under attack for fulfilling her duties at The Hospital for Sick Children in Toronto. It also reports on my efforts to save the lives of Mr. Mulatu Mekonnen and his family. He was threatened with death as the Acting President of the Ethiopian Teacher's Federation when its President had fled to the UK and his Assistant was killed in Addis Ababa. His own life was threatened in Budapest following his open discussion at an Education International Conference, which I also attended, of the dire situation at the time in Ethiopia. He and his family recently retired in Canada.

THE INSIDE WORLD
POEMS

HIS LUNG

he has an asthmatic lung
pneumonic priest   judas kiss
victim of emotion
he has a bronchiectasis
of right cardiophrenic angle
he has living and dead tissue
as sacrament   eternal tangle
beast and angel cohabit there
twin pathologies well disguised
like any normal conjugal pair
he has x-ray film
one frame of motion picture
biography of politics and love
side by side   symbiotic fate
two women's faces can be seen
freedom and the state
are there on the screen
he has two souls as Faustus said
the one is living   the other dead
the inside world is stabilized
he sees the film   there is no doubt
the outside world is just his lung
turned inside out

THREE WOODCUTS BY EDVARD MUNCH
(Haus der Kunst)

I

She waits in silence by the sea.
Her head is turned away from me.
I stand a foot or two behind,
Head bent, hand shyly wants to find
Her hand, but she it seems has none.
Our life together has begun:
"Two Human Beings" carved in wood
And finished. It is understood
That we cannot unite or sever.
Some borders here are cut forever,
Unending sea is carved before,
Behind is cut unmeasured shore.

II

"Toward the Forest" we will go,
Arms around each other now,
Into the pine trees waiting green,
The beds of grass, and we unseen
Enter a world which has no place,
No mark of time. We leave no trace
Of indecision, guilt, or care,
Where entering's for those who dare
To live outside themselves – a play,
A song, a woodcut, or ballet.
But others look in everywhere
And find that we were never there.

III

"Encounter in Space" the title reads,
And shows me naked, red, with beads
Of sweat, or are they lines of age?
Head held in hands, and inward – rage.
Nothing to clasp onto – not her.
She glides by motionless, no stir,
No outward evidence of lust,
Head balanced on her arm. My thrust
Has no defense, no welcoming.
She studies me in silence, cannot sing.
Naked and blue, yet she is there
To be encountered in despair.

FROM MY ROOM BY THE SLAUGHTERHOUSE

STAUFEN IM BREISGAU

Each morning just at seven
I'm awakened by the cries
And authoritarian acts,
The cold efficient means
Of providing for my dinner.
My bedroom window opens
On the closing down of eyes
And shuttering of screams.
Is there an animal awareness
Of what is waiting there?
A terror just before?
A coldness in the blood?
A kind of disbelief?
A shock, an insult, rage?
I've looked in animal eyes,
The answer is not clear,
But I seem to think I see
The acceptance of the State
And my own reflection there.

FLIGHT PATHS

Leaving Holland was leaving Greece once more!
Lufthansa swallowing up its daily fare
In Athens and in Amsterdam and leaping
Instrument illumined, ignorant, into arc,
Two particular paths of flight becoming
One universal arc by virtue of goal.
Human intentions break down metal barriers.
The limits of all space are self-controlled,
And moving is powered by engines of desire.
We are not transported contrariwise
By mind's eternal thought and body's want.
The limited and limiting with us is one,
Bodies are we, our flight toward the sun.

In Zeeland, and on Crete, and Mykonos
Windmill wings describe perimeters of
Aristotelian perfection, motion eternal,
Desire and limit unite, systems of
Communication binding sky and green,
Acting at a distance in between.
Earthen dikeworks limit earth desirous,
Energeia of the *dunamis* to live,
Doric columns measure wild receptive
Earth and male fertility of sun.
Particulars will universalize
In act. We bodies suffer our reversal,
Our movement together is our universal.

Sand dunes south of Scheveningen protected
Us against the sea and wind, each grain
Particular, enclosed, no conversation, we waited
Upon walls in Rijksmuseum. Is each self-portrait
Of Rembrandt particular, or do they speak together?
We wondered at facades and canon and bridges,
Ate cakes and syrup and coffee and young Genever

We bronzed in the sun of Delos and fed on oranges
And fish and sweet tomatoes in oil, and peaches
From a tin and clear strong Ouzo,
And full from seas swim lay naked on the sand
And Goddess of Delos I arced above you and we
Describing perfect perimeters of eternity
Became flight path without protection of wing,
Controlled as windmills, universal as columns,
Strong as dikeworks, explosive as twin seas,
Complete as Athens or as Amsterdam,
Particularly transformed and gone.
Expectant Leda lived through you once more
And I became Apollo whom you bore.

You were not there. You'd chosen not to come.
Our Greece held me alone amid its stones
And Holland shut me up in libraries
Among particular texts of anarchists,
But body's memory made a space for you,
Communication needs a landing place,
Turns again to aircraft wing dynamics,
Substitutes for stone. My arc completes
Its circle, perfect path of flight, to you
My goal, my ground awaiting wheel. Now
The energy is us, let us become
Windmill, dikework, column, airplane, one!

ON EDVARD MUNCH'S "SEPARATION"
(Haus der Kunst, München)

She waits in silence by the sea.
The hand not hesitating reached for joy,
Risked the early grasping after fruit,
Asserting, Augustine-aware,
In defiance of authorized acts,
Its being hand.

And in the heart treatises of hope
Were privately printed and spoken
Against the canons of practicality
Proclaiming that heart courts
No correct critics.

But heart and hand alike suffer
Sufficient precision surgery
When team of established experts
Consulting established practice
Takes up steady-stanced the scalpel.

Do treatises let speak? does fruit
Let flower the voice, the seed, of joy
Or hope of joining (unauthorized,
Impractical) when held within
The severed heart and hand?

PRIVACY

part of you lives in secret,
the other part with me,
there's a private room inside you
and you've kept from me the key,
not hidden – there it is – but
not given; that's the key
to the key

I AM KANDINSKY NOW
(Städtische Gallerie, München)

Kandinsky, you were wisest when
You hurled mountain down on moor
And set a diving cloud on fire
To celebrate a house you knew
As hers, and loved your Gabriele.

Kandinsky, was it 1910?
You lifted up the sky to lure
Tree into energy, church spire
Toward its launching pad, a few
Reminders of your Gabriele.

When you made Murnau out of linen
And bent a locomotive sure
Upon its destination higher
Than had been hoped for, was it you
Who chose to brake, or Gabriele?

I come from mountain, not from men,
Breathe moor, live spire's sharp contour,
Have locomotive's slant desire,
Ride cloud, am tree, know her house too,
But fear her choice, my Gabriele!

THE CRIME OF JOURNALIST WALLRAFF

In Syntagma Square that afternoon
After iced coffee and cool camparis
Under umbrellas, and shaded from sun,
I witnessed the crime of journalist Wallraff
Who had chained himself to a lamppost base
And was handing out leaflets describing conditions
Of workers in Athens and other Greek cities,
Of more than two thousand prisoners in jails,
While smiling tourists stopped to take pictures
Of the man who was rival to columns and stones,
As if all arranged by the Office of Tourism,
When suddenly <u>Dike</u> who avenges excesses
Required the leaflets by dashing his head
To the pavement and splintering his glasses
Into thousands of visions of shattered worlds
Where freedom lies handcuffed behind his back.
And <u>Dike</u> with vengeance supplied State bootery
To stomach and genitals and spat in the face
That dared to look up, and stepped on his eyes
With full weight of <u>Ananke</u>, authorized,
And stopped his screams with a shoe in his mouth
Until it was clear he came close to strangling
On properly polished and promulgated leather.
Taken away with a chain around his neck,
He was sentenced to one-year-and-two-months in prison
Without right of appeal. So here is his appeal,
Written in lines that won't last, on the back
Of the catalogue of the National Museum.

I met in German factories,
As undercover reporter, Greeks.
I learned their character, learned to love Greece,
Learned their fear of reprisals. Fear
Of joining workers' groups. Fear
Of criticizing their State. Fear
Of arrest when they returned. Fear
For families left behind. Examine
Entrance of underground garage,
Central Police Number Four, odos-
Meganon, by American Embassy. Examine
Blood-stained bench, blood-spattered wall,
Outermost corner left, prisoners there
Strapped to bench, beaten with cudgels
And whips by six to ten bulls. Examine
Interrogation Bureau, odos-Messaljiou,
Where students are collected from street and home
Without warrant of arrest or legal protection.
Examine shock-torture cells in Piraeus.
Examine the prison-island of Jaros . . .

The crime of which Wallraff is convicted:
Violation of paragraph number one,
Of the latest Military Constitution,
4 and 17 / 11 / '73, to wit:
"The dignity of man is inviolable.
To respect and protect it is the duty of State.
Propaganda against the Greek Nation is forbidden.
To publish information is also forbidden
Which incites in the People fear and unrest."

The terrible crime of journalist Wallraff,
Handing out leaflets in Syntagma Square,
Is also judged in foreign journals
Which fail to report of tyranny and torture
And terror in Greece and other lands:
'Publicity Gag!' 'Self-martyrdom!'
'Illegal interference in the affairs of a State!'
<u>Dike</u> and <u>Ananke</u> have again combined
To punish all people of the Wallraff kind
Whose actions and speech cannot be confined
By fiends of the State whose gods are blind,
Whose names are forever consigned to the wind.

Pallas Athena
Athena Parthenos
blessed virgin
pure aether and stormcloud
twilight and dawn
goddess of counsel
goddess of war
goddess of womanly industry and art
Athena Polias
protectress of cities
Athena Nike
bringer of victory
Hear him speak!
Hear and strike!

And it calls on you, oh gods and tourists,
To leave your iced coffees under umbrellas
And strike! Strike in the name of all human
Bodies rotting like meat in cells
Of immortal cities' two thousand hells.
Strike in the name of Günter Wallraff,
A journalist beaten and thrown into jail
For the crime of handing out leaflets whose tale
Was of persons beaten and thrown into jail.

Αθηνά

HAUPTBAHNHOF MÜNCHEN

Your hand from my hand at precisely 18.09 – – – – –

>   when you on platform and I
>   in train through open window stretched
>   together fingers connecting fingers
>
>   when without public announcement
>   the seven month trip was precisely described
>   on ticket: Einfach Bern / Zweite Klasse
>
>   when the precise moment arrived
>   and station grey and wrinkled as engineers'
>   elbows blurred in my eyes
>
>   when arms which had held what they were grown for
>   hung from window like empty mail bags
>   not knowing the time of their next collection
>
>   when thighs that long kept warmth together
>   with thighs were fixed at a distance
>   by timetable's gravitation and
>   were cold steel rails bolted to wood
>
>   when the precise moment arrived
>   dividing perception and memory into
>   separate compartments without reservation
>   as smoker from non-smoker: choice of habits

when iron feet under me awoke and began to
        move with far less drama and import than
        is met before wurst and beer stands
        or in the public toilets

when you were yet warm on my mouth
        and you faded into photographs
        as unceremoniously as D-Mark
        into Swiss Franc is exchanged

when the precise moment arrived
        and instantly between arrival and departure
        something was found again like luggage
        sent to the wrong destination and recovered

when in that hand-holding-finger-coupling-moment
        it became impossible for us to part

                                        – – – – parted.

IN THE MENSA, BERN

I'm sitting in the mensa
eating cold potatoes,
undetected and not
expectedly composing
verse on a serviette, my
thin defense against damage,
protecting pants. I know that
you're at home now reading
the letter that I wrote you
some days ago in the mensa
while eating cold potatoes.
Making love by mail's like
balancing food on a fork, the
chance is in the opening.
I'm sending my only defenses,
verse on a serviette,
not waiting for your answer,
leaving unprotected cold
potatoes, pants, and me.

AUDEN'S SLIPPERS
(For Emily, Clare, Chris, Jackie, Kirsten)

Auden wore slippers wherever he went,
Which sparked curiosity, but rarely resent.
Working on <u>Poetic Edda</u> with Peter Salus in Toronto
He wanted 'dim sum' for his mid-day meal to share
With Peter and me, our wives, and the family there.
He was charming with the children and very wise,
And he loved the delight he saw in their eyes.
"Why do you wear slippers?" they asked out of care
And concern for the great man who was their guest.
"Because my corns ache," he replied, impressed.
"Slippers are best when feet need to heal."
Then all settled down to our Chinese meal.

He read, at the University, some recent poems,
And addressed the questions about what he wrote.
His slippers were evident, but no one took note.
In the presence of greatness they wished to be seen
For their self-conscious probes, and self-esteem,
Whereas Auden, well-slippered, quietly laughed,
And stuck to his well-honed craft.

HEADLINE

when
I read
<u>The Daily Depress</u>
I
appreciate
all
the more
that
one hears
of Canada
less

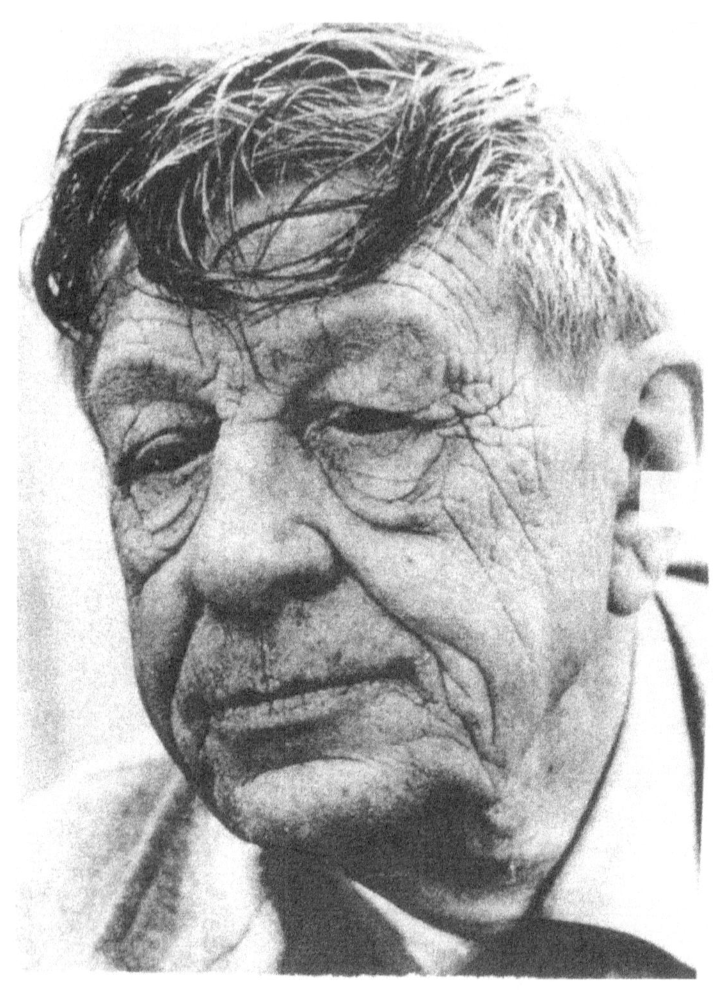

Wystan Auden, Poetic Mentor

AT DUSK
(To remember Wystan Auden,
Poetic Mentor)

It is dusk. *Die Götterdämmerung* is near.
The World is in love with death and fear.
Everywhere wars and brutal killing;
Evidence of Peace finds no fulfilling.
The Owl of Minerva, as Hegel foresaw,
Spreads its wings with the gathering of dusk,
And Wagner provided the musical thrust.
The gods themselves, he said, must die.
The outside world resumes its natural state,
And Humankind faces its own fate.

Systems of domination mark the foundation
Of every contemporary nation:
Race, gender, income, sexual orientation,
All rooted in supremacy, and sustained
By legal practice and official confirmation.
The politicians are lying! Democracy is dying!
Our political-economic plight has given flight
To the predatory forces of the night.

What do we see at the gathering of dusk?
Humankind putting the Earth off course.
We are the animal species that needs
Other species to need us, if even by force,
For friendship or for exploitation: the template,
Or paradigm, of course, to treat our own species.
We give ourselves leave to live by desire,
Forcing all species, to work for hire,
Not relating our means to ethical ends
We disrupt the social balance that Aristotle intends.

At dusk we see the high priests we now know:
Financiers, monopolists, rentiers all in a row
Adding nothing of value, or productive – not labour –
To amass unearned income from asset gains
While seizing the political and economic reins.
The non-democratic one percent – oligarchic and
Authoritarian who privatize the land,
Education, natural resources and more.
For Neoliberal control of the ninety-nine, and the poor.
If democracy and socialism threaten their might,
They persuade the public not to fight
For better wage labour or equal right.

At dusk Philosophy should spread its wings.
Medicine acts on outside world things
To aid and to heal our bodies and brains.
Philosophy is the medicine of the inside world
Where animal species are left with their pains.
Philosophy, when it spreads its wings,
Needs Poetry as Illumination of our life's state –
Or, as Alchemy of the Inside World – to liberate
Our thoughts, feelings, and dreams that create
And motivate our lives and actions and cares
To protect us from outside world evil snares.

'Poetry makes nothing happen,' said Auden laconic:
Create political parties or markets economic,
Or defeat the contemporary forces demonic.
But Philosophy could as a Way of Life that redeems
If inspired by Auden's illumination aims and means.
A Way of Life can oppose strife, and act as it should
For Truth, Good, and what we must change.
Nothing else has the adequate necessary range.

A luminous Philosophy integrates our lived-in world,
Alienated by force and foresight, with hate unfurled
In a people and a nation where wrong is made right:
Dusk is a moment before the darkness of Night –
Just a moment to re-integrate and to foresee
What a Person is – and is for – and must be:
A being whose being is being for others, related
Reciprocally, and responsible, for all human beings,
In harmony with nature and other species,
The dusk becomes light if we redeem the night.
We create our relevance through our benevolence.

But that remains to be tested. We cannot stay rested.
It may seem far away, and we cannot catch a breath.
How can We and our Earth survive the forces of Death?
And what did Hegel in his time really foresee?
What is the Owl of Minerva's life expectancy?

GOOD NIGHT SWEET LOVE
(On reading Drayton's Sonnet XXXVII)

Good night sweet love, the morning does not dare
To break the force that holds us two as one
Or interrupt the rivers just begun
To flow together with its fear and care.

Morning offers simple soaring things
That warmly yield to tender touch and kiss
But cannot hold the mood that follows this
And is replaced by gods with heavy wings.

For Domination governs every day
Authority must have a firm control
And Power will not dissolve into the whole
Until all oligarchs are swept away.

Freedom has its logic, as Bakunin said,
Destructive urges are creative too
Resistance precedes rest for me and you.
No more good nights until the State is dead.

Executed January 1919 Berlin

By German Freicorps Troops

Under GKSD Orders

ON SOCIALISM

It was killed in the womb at seven months,
Before its expected birth in Greece of freedom,
Hope, and magic alchemy, a conception in the
Minds of men, and a lonely London library.

Father, new world's hopeful hunger, wolf certain,
Full as the morning was near, looked on with
Eyes unable to see what eyes were built to see:
Matters of history, unromantic empiricist he.

Mother, old Germany's proxy, grown practical,
Who bore and nurtured in pain democracy,
Skeptical she, critic of wolves and anarchists and
Insecurity, willfully decides the time to abort.

The end in neutral Zurich, of insurance firms,
Was simple and quiet, as suits an unborn:
No last words, nor even regret; and a question
Unasked: woman's right, or was it murder?

Father, wrapped in old overcoat the remains,
Returned to improbable capital Bern, where
Is buried Bakunin of unfulfilled hopes,
And labored as usual, impractical, on reasons.

Mother, baggage long packed by financiers,
Turned a face forgetful to the evening sky.
To the State, secure and unfree, a father who
Would guarantee a Neo-Liberal pregnancy.

VOYAGES

They came from northern ranges,
They crossed the northern seas
through time-zone changes
of tenths of centuries;
through space-curve encounters
with finite boundaries:
revelations of Themselves,
promises of perfection
and images of destinies.
She was His Mirror, She
who saw Her own reflection
not.

Once They stood on Spanish strand,
strange as Islam in court of Alhambra.
(Lā ilāhu illá lláh!)
spanish gold in the golden sand
by San Pedro de Alcantará.
    ¿Donde tu eres, ma bella?
    Marbella, Marbella, Marbella.
    Where are You now, my gold?
    Where are You now, my golden
    one?

They set sail from São Vicente
to navigate Their souls, and bent
over helm, drove Their ships afar.
Having learned Portuguese navigation
He charted course by His true star
and discovered a constellation
on the waves below Alvor.
>   Erque-te ó sol de verão!
>   Portimão, Portimão, Portimão.
>   True star are You now?
>   True star, will You now
>   be true?

They scanned Istanbul through its mud,
encountered its fires at every turn.
On waves of plunder fires return,
from Ravenna to Beyoğlu They burn.
Icons of movement, fire and mud,
sailed them back to Byzantium
where sang in His arms His golden bird
as in boughs of the gardens of sultans.
>   Öğün, güven, Topkapi sarayi!
>   Aksaray! Aksaray! Aksaray!
>   the dolmuş cry. My golden bird,
>   where did You fly?
>   Why did You fly
>   away?

Voyages find harbor in feeling,
infinite boundaries revealing
what Mirror turned inward is concealing:
that voyages find no perfection.
Photos alone remain for reflection,
left over strands of remembered lands,
the inside world is held in our hands.

Mirror, can you reflect our relation?
If you are true star and I constellation
Golden bird may fly in my arms most free
Voyager, shall we sail together
Into rough seas and calmer weather?
True star, will you now be true
To me?

THE LEAF THAT FROM THAT TREE

The leaf that from that tree
Shot out green, impatient
For unfolding, and hung above
Hyena eyes and thrash of
Traffic into summer's airborne,
Bending atmospherically with
Pressure, has today without
Ever hurting someone else
Parachuted forever to earth.

HERACLES TO HIS TENURE COMMITTEE

Horrible Hydra, haunter of swamps,
Of sacred groves by the river banks,
Of spaces where the Muses go,
Are you waiting there to menace me?
How many snake-like heads do you
Prepare for venomous bite? Euripedes
Tells of ten thousand. Apollodorus
Pausanius, Diodorus, Simonides,
Say a college of priestesses full,
Or one hundred, like the centuriae,
Or nine to celebrate fair Semele.
Seven have I seen on drachmae, and believe
Seven are sufficient when one is immortal.
There in your tracks waits death. Alone
The scent of them can kill, I'm told;
And destruction is on your breath. How then
Shall I send up fiery arrows to call
You into the open? How hold my breath?
When you coil at my feet to make me fall,
How shall I hammer your heads to fibres?
With what? And what would I win if new heads
From those already crushed bulge up?
No club have I, no defenses, no sword,
No golden falchion to carve away
From your dog-like body its immortal head;

And how without weapon shall I disembowel you?
And how shall I crack the well-rumored crab
Come dishonestly to pinch at my heel?
Murderous monster! I have no such weapons.
No Iolus have I at my call with chariot
Swift-wheeled for help in lighting fires
In the groves, for help in cauterizing pulp
Of heads destroyed to prevent new growths.
And if an Iolus I had, I have
No doubt my labours would not count,
Were I to win, but be disqualified.
Although I know you are there, I fear
To fare no better than the traveler
Who journeys out full of joy, and – trusting
His honest labours and pure intent
Will win him through to evening meal,
To shelter and much needed rest – wanders
Without knowing into your den of death.
Horrible Hydra, are you there?
Come, then, appear! Here am I,
No weapon in hand, and without defense,
With nine years hard work to show, and weary,
With truth, and renewed demands of right.
Come! Here am I, a creature of needs,
A speaker of words and a doer of deeds.

DECEMBER

given on birthday
scented candles and wines
tasty apples and pears
and Benedictines
and omelettes
and coffees
      a candle is lit
      and it glows

given on Christmas
sugary cakes with allures
sweet almonds and walnuts
and marillen liqueurs
and mandarin oranges
and teas
      a cake is eaten
      and it fills

given on Sylvester
rich cookies and candies
dried apricots and figs
and soothing brandies
and jellies of quince
and hot glüh-wines
        a brandy is sipped
        and it warms

given today
to celebrate
a day
not noted before
love
        love is given and oh
        oh it is loved
        and wants more

INCARNATION

Nothing is so lonely as a Christmas tree
in a room without children
except, of course, for philosophy
which lives alone now under the roof
an old man in an old overcoat . . .
this isn't an age for him
doesn't measure, doesn't predict
isn't sociology
isn't peripatetic
isn't up with his ancestors . . .
there were real candles on our tree
and without glasses we could see
what Parmenides said must Be
we saw being, oneness, truth
justice, beauty, ideology
we saw the being of man
more than methodology
we saw freedom and dignity
we saw god and rebellion
we saw life valued over theory . . .
but philosophy – growing old, and cold, and
the children having all left home –
has artificial needs, lacks energy
cannot live without glasses, cannot see
not without glasses and electricity . . .
and an old overcoat

FAUST STUBE

From the hillsides of Staufenberg down
Into streets of Staufen come warm summer winds,
Sweet scents of grape growing vines
Combine on lips that smile, part, and shine,
Whetted with summer's festival wine
Music and chatter fill the square,
Dancing is also there.

Beside Faust Stube is found
One place still free.
Filtered through wine glass round
He sees with surprise her green-grey eyes,
Then were they acquainted forever,
Conjured dreams, clasped hands together,
By August alchemy in Black Forest green
They changed into each other's being.

There lived Dr. Faustus too, it is said,
Who tried to conjure gold from lead.
His alchemy had failed, and he was dead.
Where love and life are not concealed,
Through Poetry they are revealed.
Where action at a distance can take the field,
Poetry is the alchemy of the inside world.

TRAFFIC

we're living inside of posters
we're reproduced
we're printed flat on the surface
we're two-dimensional
we've taken our points and lines inside
we're under cover of colors
posters are our cathedrals

posters for travel   for sales
for tales and trials   for elections
for propaganda   posters for politics
labor posters   posters for government
advertising posters   posters for sex

posters are not important   but
their reproduction is
we're living inside of posters
we're not important   but
we're easy to reduplicate

reproduction is control
time was when rationality
meant understanding of control
logos measured by what-is
now rationality means
control of understanding
Heraclitus does not exist
the constant is not change
but measured pace of change
perfected   timed   controlled

not production but reproduction
Marx was wrong   we're not producers
the important question is
who controls the means of reproduction?
birth control is reproduction
who controls that?
News is reproduction
who controls news?
who controls government?
who controls change?
who controls traffic?

it is amazing to consider
the controlled flow of traffic
not to change with traffic
is to hurt the pride of mayors
not to acknowledge posters
angers the urban guerillas

wet streets are like newspapers
they reproduce traffic
lights flash into them and out
cameras record only ribbons
parliaments and congresses are wet streets
political speeches are wet streets
commercial ads are wet streets
birth control devices are wet streets
through wet streets march armies
anonymous heads   voices disconnected
howl with headlines and die in their birth

birth control is traffic
controlled
capital is traffic
controlled
government is traffic
controlled
and all offices and parties
and parliamentary acts and votes
communism is traffic
controlled
certainly private property
was born in traffic

we're born in traffic too
we're living inside of posters
we're reproduced
we're printed flat on the surface
we're two-dimensional
we've taken our points and lines inside
we're under cover of colors
posters are our cathedrals

River Aare

HIGH ABOVE AARE: A LOVE SONG

He wanders with sun down waking street,
Shadows, ancient overcoats of Bern, retreat
To rationality of time from Zytglockturm,
Baring morning songs in stone, public buildings,
Bringing to light a renaissance of fountains:
Samson, Justice, Bear in armor, Ape, Moses,
Bagpiper, Eater of Small Children. These
Personify blood forces, sunk deeply into cells
Like well springs sunk into earth where sunlight
Never seeps – waters rushing up, then returning.
Desire, not sun, lights up his morning.

Celebrations serve for songs at lauds,
Shop windows under the arcades in Spital-, Markt-,
And Gerechtigkeitsgassen discover to revelers
A litany of cakes and chocolates, cheese
And fruit pies, and sausages and toys. The pilgrims
Find their way past rows of flower vendors.
Through onion stalls explodes the sun at midday,
High above Aare, Cathedral wants God.
He waits below, a catechumen outside his sources.
He puts on vestments God has not yet worn,
His desire was old before the Church was born.

He stations himself upon the grosse Schanze,
He meditates on night when, freed from sun's
Rival glare and bright, he can return again
To sacraments, when fountains no longer serve
As saints of Becoming, when bodies without shadows
Blend with stone, when souls without walls walk free,
When hands not well defined by light hold Her
As Cathedral spire at night without light holds God,
When distance is neither space nor time but energy,
When desire becomes his only stability
He is fixed on Aare's roiling watery surge
That sparks desire's ardent poetic urge,
A Love Song to his Beloved truthfully
Expressing their mutually shared humanity.
Transmuted by muse Erato's alchemy,
The Inside meaning of Love Song must be
To treat each living thing benevolently.

WYSTAN HUGH AUDEN – IN MEMORIAM
(For Peter H. Salus)

Wystan Auden, with what pride
Dawned the day on which you died!
September twenty-nine, Nineteen seventy-three.
Aged sixty-six, in old Vienna.
It was sixty-six degrees that day,
And partly cloudy. W. B. Yeats, you say,
Disappeared in the dead of winter.
And all the instruments agree, you say
That the day of his death was a dark cold day.

Was your departure day cold and dark?
No. The instruments do not agree that the death
Of a poet must be kept from his poems, or
Consecrated to unearthly things. Not so.
Double header (Mets and Cubs)
Rained out in New York City; and
Agnew declares in Washington that he
Will not resign if he's indicted.
Russian two-man space flight is successful;
Waters off Greece are dangerously polluted;
And Dalai Lama wants to meet the Pope.
Rumanian Travel Bureau to begin
A Dracula Tour in the months ahead,
And Germany thinks of publishing the
Secret diary of Joseph Goebbels.
In Vienna, a storm of protest
Against a government decision
To close off transit for Soviet Jews
Using Austria to emigrate to Israel.
In New York a fuel crisis warning,
And 121 tennis courts are
Slated for resurfacing.

In Kirchstaetten we meet again
When Peter and I drove tree-lined lane
To where you lived. Just one year ago,
September, Nineteen seventy-two.
We sat and talked before noon meal
Until it was time to drive to town for
Milk that Chester needed for dinner.

You talked over midday meal of poetry
And music, and played the phonograph.
In the garden you read your latest poem.

One week before, on Sunday
September twenty-third, died
The Poet Pablo Neruda,
Twelve days after the murder of his friend
Salvador Allende, and after
The burial of democracy in Chile,
In spite of surrealism and politics,
In spite of poetry and alchemy.
Was that day too a dark cold day?

Wystan Auden, today is the day
You join the poets of our age
You tell your friends you're going away
To look for poems and acts of courage

What do your instruments combine to say?
Poetry makes nothing happen, you contend,
But poetry happens in us. We change.
Politics leaves everything the same
But poetry is an alchemy, reserved
For transformation from base conditions
Of living souls to things of value.
Without such alchemy there is no soul;
There is no love, just politics.
There is no questing without poetry,
And nothing is divine. It's true, of course,
Vice-Presidents can be indicted without
Poetry, and space ships launched,
And water polluted without poetry.
Without poetry Goebbels' diary can appear,
And Jews locked up inside of Russia;
And tennis courts can be resurfaced.
A poet can die without the aid of poetry,
And even without a dark cold day.
Poetry is not history, to be sure;
History like politics, is quite dismembered,
Without poetry nothing is remembered.

And what for memories there yet shall be
Wait upon poems like yours to foresee.
What will there be then to celebrate
When future Septembers can liberate
The souls of poets? Will people hear
The words of poets sounding there?
Or is that just the hollow sound
Of tennis balls upon resurfaced ground?

CITIZEN AND PRESIDENT

Auden's Epitaph in Westminster Abbey

"In the deserts of the heart
Let the healing fountain start
In the prison of his days
Teach the free man how to praise."

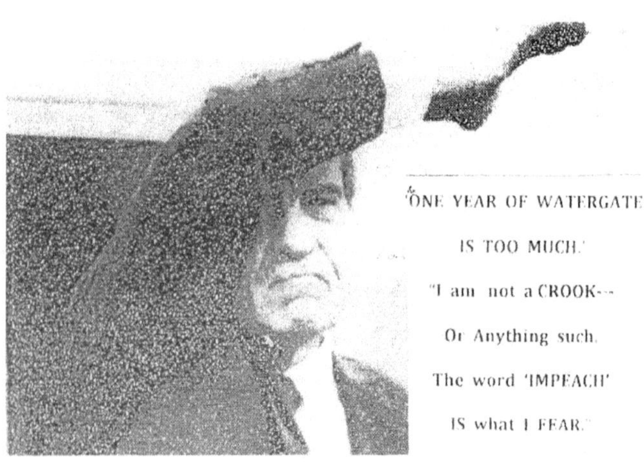

W.H. AUDEN – THE POET OF DEMOCRATIC CITIZENSHIP

We may not be aware, on first reading W. H. Auden, how much attention he devotes to the subject of Human Persons and their Political and Social relations. It is one of the things that attracted me to Auden from the beginning. Now, more than fifty years after his death in 1973, Auden is more significant and relevant in our era than before he died, even though he had become one of the most important English language poets of the twentieth century.

Animals other than humans need not be concerned with politics. For human beings, however, it is a must concern. Auden once mused: "Walked through the woods; saw the birds in the trees. They had no politicians and sang at their ease. They weren't the human race, my dear; they weren't the human race." He said that humans were the political race, and that Democracy was the natural politics for Human Beings, especially since the historical dominance of Capitalism and Fascism.

"Democracy," he wrote, "cannot be genuine unless each of us, in his or her sphere, is prepared to serve it with heart and head." And "each . . . has a political duty nobody else can perform." It must be by means of active and voluntary participation in public affairs. Each individual must be educated, well-informed and rational; and capable of distinguishing good from bad for making political and social decisions to improve their social, democratic environment. He identified the positive individual human attributes as critical consciousness, creativity, and communal cooperation. He was critical of the current state of education, however, and the lack of commitment of individuals to engaging in communal matters. He described a democratic life as "a life of love and affection among ordinary happy people, a life which capitalism, specialisation, and over academic education are still making extremely difficult." In his poem 'The Unknown Citizen,' he satirized the sort of citizen who was perfectly obedient, passive, and uncritical: "He served the

Greater Community . . . he paid his dues . . . his reactions . . . were normal in every way . . . he was fully insured . . . . Our researchers are content that he held the proper opinions. When there was peace, he was for peace; when there was war, he went to war."

Human Beings, Auden believed, are born neither free nor good. They are social animals. Each individual is the product of a social life. They continue their evolution through the use of conscious intelligence to exercise freedom and goodness on an experiential basis rather than to simply follow orders, or to adapt to the environment. Humans have the power to control and change it. Democracy is the most characteristic manifestation of humanity. Citizens are not merely 'groups' of humans, nor what is sometimes called 'the middle class.' Living together in a community with the inherent interest and will to improve the community in which they live is what makes individuals into citizens. Active participation in the organizing and well-being of their community is what the democratic citizens do.

It has become the usual practice of most political and social media (TV and newspapers and broadcasts) in the USA, Canada, and elsewhere to win public interest by concentrating their commentaries on the politically powerful and well-known leaders – presidents, prime ministers and party bosses, etc. – rather than on ordinary democratic citizens. When Auden rather suddenly died away from home in 1973, the internal political climate was less imbued with strict authoritarianism than it has become in the last 50 years. In the USA Republican Richard Nixon was president. His time in office was overshadowed by what became known as "The Watergate Scandal" in which members of the Committee to Re-elect the President (appropriately named 'Creeps') assisted Nixon in breaking into the Democratic National Committee for espionage and sabotage, installing bugging devices. G. Gordon Liddy and James McCord were convicted of conspiracy and burglary. Nixon lied and proclaimed "I am not a CROOK!" But his secret White House tapes came to light, and he was impeached by the House Judiciary Committee. He remarked, "I know you heard what you thought I said, but what I said was not what I meant"; and "I didn't do anything wrong, and I promise never to do it again." Nixon, known broadly as 'Tricky Dick,' resigned as President the following year, August 9, 1974. W.H. Auden, who remarked that his education in the United Kingdom was tarnished with Fascism, had become a citizen of the USA on May 20, 1964. But he had always refused to support President Richard Nixon because he had contempt for Nixon's secretive authoritarianism which he thought undermined democratic citizenship.

Now, fifty years later, we have entered the era of Donald Trump in the USA and Vladimir Putin in Russia. Neither leader has claimed to be democratic in his approach to rule. Together they have created a New World Order; and it isn't a democratic one. Both are Autocrats with the support of sizable Oligarchies which Auden always despised. Donald Trump, after surviving death threats, proclaimed that "God saved my life so that I could Make America Great Again." US President Joe Biden, in his 'Farewell Address' to the American people, emphasized the unfortunate wide-spread growth of Oligarchy in America since the time of President Eisenhower who had warned about the power of the 'Military-Industrial Complex.'

The questions Auden would surely pose now are: 'can citizen democracy survive these extreme forms of authoritarian rule?' And. 'just what is the role and duty of citizens?' If democracy is the most characteristic manifestation of humanity, as Auden says, then democratic human citizens cannot become passive, self-satisfied, powerless, silent and selfish beings ignorant of their own needs and the needs of other living beings (animal and human). For Auden a democratic citizen has a Voice. And persons with voices must use those voices to participate in ensuring the well-being of their communities and habitats. It may include working for change, diversity, equality, and inclusion to support truth, freedom and the good life. Do not run away from extreme autocracy! Run toward it! Refuse to accept it! That is what Alexei Navalny did by returning to Russia after being poisoned by Putin. It is also what Martin Luther King did, in the face of assassination threats after his 1963 March on Washington and 'I Have a Dream' speech. He was assassinated in Memphis , Tennessee. while planning 'The Poor People's Campaign' in 1968. It is what Auden's democratic citizens must do also when faced with the poisons and threats of a Trumpian New World Order.

W.H. Auden's most personal and expressive voice was, of course, Poetry. He said that poets "do not invent new thoughts or feelings . . . their skills with words . . . crystallise and define with greater precision the thoughts and feelings which are generally present . . . and may illuminate . . . but will not dictate." Poetry, as Auden understands it, is 'Illumination:' i.e., Insight and Awareness. And it has the power to "disturb" and "elucidate." It has a humanizing potential.

> All I have is a voice
> To undo the folded lie, . . .
> And the lie of Authority . . .
> There is no such thing as the State
> And no one exists alone; . . .
> We must love one another or die.
> Defenseless under the night
> Our world in stupor lies;
> Yet, dotted everywhere,
> Ironic points of light
> Flash out . . .
> May I, composed like them . . .
> Beleaguered by the same
> Negation and despair,
> Show an affirming flame.

ABOUT THE AUTHOR

William Clarence Graham was born in Cleveland, Ohio in 1934 and moved, with his family, to Los Angeles, California at the age of six where his father, an engineer, had been commissioned a Naval officer to oversee the construction of war ships during World War II. As the son of an officer he was offered a chance to take sailing courses, an opportunity which would play a huge role in his life to the present day. He attended the private Jesuit-run Loyola High School until 1952; then Loyola University (B.S. Cum Laude, 1956; M.A. Literature and Philosophy, 1958; and induction into Alpha Sigma Nu International Scholastic Honors Society). It was as a student of Literature that he began writing poetry under the influence of his admiration for the poetry of W.H. Auden whom he 'adopted' as his mentor. He began teaching Literature at Loyola, and Philosophy at UCLA where he studied advanced Logic under Carnap and VonWright.

Graham went to Canada to earn a M.A. in Philosophy at the University of Toronto in 1962. Needing to support his young family, he returned to Los Angeles to teach Literature and Philosophy as Asst. Prof. at Mt. St. Mary's College, and formed a W.H. Auden reading society in L.A. In 1965 he went to the University of Toronto again as a George Paxton Young Fellow and Lecturer to complete work on his Ph.D. in Philosophy (Thesis: "Strawson's Concept of a Person," 1969) under the mentorship of Emil Fackenheim and C.B. Macpherson. He was offered a variety of professorships in the US at Univ. California and the Ivy League Brown and Temple Universities. But he decided to accept a professorship at University of Toronto, both because of the stability he sought for his family, as well as the opportunity he was offered to become the first full-time Philosopher at the recently founded U. of T. satellite Campus in Scarborough. The Principal, Wynne Plumptre, appointed him to head the Chair of the General Policy Committee to oversee development of the Campus (1966 – 1970). He was also Acting Chair of the Division of

Humanities in 1970. A short time later he was offered the position of Vice Principal and Registrar of U. of T. Scarborough. He declined.

U. of T. President Claude Bissel struck a 'Presidential Committee on the Status and Future of Scarborough College,' (1970 – 1971) to which the Scarborough faculty members elected Graham. He was promoted to Associate Professor with Tenure in 1975 and full Professor in 1991. He was contracted by the Foundation for the Improvement of Post Secondary Education (FIPSE) for problems at the University of Southern Mississippi (1986 – 1989).

When Graham was called up for Tenure at U. of T. he not only submitted evidence of his teaching ability and his growing list of academic publications, he also submitted (at the request of the Committee) examples of the poetry he had continued to write. He then composed a poem especially for the occasion (included in this volume, as "Heracles to His Tenure Committee"). Being granted tenure led Graham to also become a citizen of Canada, making him a dual citizen, which he is to the present.

His close friend and mentor C.B. Macpherson, who was President of the Canadian Association of University Teachers, argued that U. of T. professors and their Faculty Association (UFTA), had ineffective labour rights, collective bargaining and dispute resolution. Graham took up the challenge of UTFA, and was elected President in 1992.

As President of UTFA Graham sought more stability for the Faculty Association. Judge Alan Gold, Chief Justice of the Superior Court of Quebec, was appointed Arbitrator. And he ruled in favour of the Faculty Association, allowing UTFA to finance itself adequately with dues, clearer negotiation and bargaining prowess and dispute resolution, all with the aid of labour law support (Sack Goldblatt Mitchell).

While serving eight years as President of UTFA (1992 – 2000), he was also elected President of the Ontario Confederation of University Faculty Associations (OCUFA). And when Bob Rae was elected Premier of Ontario (1990 – 1995) he summoned Graham to be an Advisor to his government and to Richard Allen as Minister of Colleges and Universities. Graham served Premier Rae on the Broadhurst Task Force on Accountability, the Minister's Round Table on Post-Secondary Education, the Council of Ministers of Education of Canada (CMEC), as well as Chair of the Delegation to Education International in Washington, DC, and as the Canadian Delegate to UNESCO. He continued to work with UNESCO for many years, and also with the Canadian Association of University Teachers (CAUT). He was elected as President of CAUT in 1998. He continued, all along, to write both poetry and philosophy.

Graham spent 1995 at Harvard University Law School's Program in Dispute Resolution and worked in Mediation Services in Massachusetts' Courts and has continued to offer mediation, negotiation and dispute resolution services in Canada since then.

In the 1990s Nancy Olivieri, a Professor of Medicine at the Hospital for Sick Children (HSC) and the University of Toronto, was caring for patients with the rare congenital blood disease of thalassimia. She became embroiled in one of the world's most notable and publicized cases of academic freedom and research integrity involving the use of drugs. Her case drew the interest of John le Carré who was writing *The Constant Gardener*, a novel about issues in the pharmaceutical industry. He interviewed Dr. Olivieri at HSC and included her in his book.

In the 1980s the standard treatment for thalassimia was deferoxamine (Deferal) which required daily inoculations to remove excess iron from patients' organs, a procedure not easy for patients to tolerate, especially if they were children. Another drug, Deferiprone (LA 01), taken orally, showed some potential. Prior to licensing by the Food and Drug Administration (FDA), however, there needed to be tests to ensure that the drug was both effective and safe. In 1988 Dr. Olivieri, with temporary funding from the Medical Research Council (MRC), became the principal investigator of Deferiprone. Over the next few years she began to have concerns about liver toxicity caused by the drug. In 1993 Dr. Gideon Koren, CIBC Research Chair at HSC introduced Dr. Olivieri to Apotex Pharmaceutical and its President Barry Sherman who agreed to produce Deferiprone and to partially fund the testing.

Apotex was Canada's largest pharmaceutical company, and Barry Sherman was estimated by the *New York Times* to be one of Canada's wealthiest persons. He had offered to donate $12.7 million to fund a research centre at the University of Toronto. As a result of the shenanigans reported here he said that he would drop the donation to $600,000. And Dr. Olivieri also suffered the consequences. The University of Toronto leadership and many of the staff wanted to keep a donor and his money happy, and sided with Sherman. So did some leaders of HSC. The very institutions that should normally have protected her academic freedom, her legal rights, and her research integrity, abandoned her. Only a few loyal friends at HSC and the Canadian Association of University Teachers (CAUT), under President William Graham and Exec. Dir. James Turk, came to her aid, as well as supporting and protecting her. President Graham intervened heavily for Dr. Olivieri with U. of T. President Robert Pritchard.

Over the next few years Dr. Olivieri began to have increased concerns about Deferiprone (LA 01), specifically about potential reduction in long-term effectiveness and increases in hepatic iron concentrations. By 1996 Apotex claimed that it did not agree with Olivieri, and Sherman did not want her to inform patients and their families about her concerns. Olivieri, in response, outlined her concerns to the Research Ethics Board. Apotex immediately terminated the trials and threatened to sue her.

Dr. Gideon Koren continued to attempt to mediate between Dr. Olivieri and Apotex, and Apotex continued its substantial funding of Dr. Koren's own research. In response Koren also published his own findings, in opposition to Dr. Olivieri, that LA 01 was effective and safe. Apotex appointed a fake panel to support its position that there was no basis for concerns. Dr. Olivieri noted that liver biopsies indicated an accelerated progression to fibrosis. Dr. Ross Cameron of Toronto analyzed the liver histology and in 1997 Dr. Olivieri, acting on his analysis, concluded that liver toxicity was caused by LA 01. She also stopped prescribing it to her HSC patients and recommended continuation of their biopsies.

It was established, by forensic evidence, that two documents produced by Gideon Koren for Professor Arnold Naymark were fabrications created in order to discredit Dr. Olivieri and to harm her professional reputation. A detective named Mr. Bone also proved, by analyzing DNA on stamped envelopes sent to Dr. Olivieri's friends, colleagues and employers, that the numerous pieces of anonymous hate mail sent to her supporters from October 1998 to May 1999 originated with Koren, and that they were meant to destroy her reputation and relationships. They were also intended to have her fired from her position of Professor of Medicine at the University of Toronto. Koren's own research, entitled "Mother Risk," which analyzed women's hair samples, was also being held up to critical professional review. He was suspended by HSC for gross misconduct, and his endowed named chair was removed. He was ordered to make restitution, but he left Canada instead.

The Canadian Association of University Teachers (CAUT) which supported Dr. Nancy Olivieri in her ordeal, commissioned a team of prominent independent experts to make a study of the entire case in 2001: "The Olivieri Report" was the result. We can now conclude that Nancy Olivieri is safely a permanent member of the Faculty of Medicine at the University of Toronto, where she continues her work on hemoglobin and cares for her adopted daughter Allegra.

In another case, Graham attended an Education International Symposium in Budapest (1999) where he heard Mr. Mulatu Mekonnen, Acting President of the Ethiopian Teachers Union describe the negative conditions of education in his country even though he had been warned not to do so before he left Addis Ababa. (The previous President had been forced to escape to England to save his life, and the Vice Pres. was gunned down in Addis Ababa.) Mulatu was warned in Budapest not to return to Ethiopia. He sought help from the US delegation with sympathy but no help. Graham was determined to save Mulatu's life. With the help of his Assistants in Ottawa, Graham was able to get him a visa and travel documents to Canada. In Canada Mulatu was granted exile and has led a good, and safe, working life with the Ontario Secondary Teachers. We were also able to get Mulatu's wife, Bethlehem, and children out of Ethiopia and safely to Canada to join him.

Graham has also served as Visiting Professor in Munich, Germany; in Bern, Switzerland; and Athens, Greece. He received a Certification of Mediation and Dispute Resolution from Harvard Law School. He spent two years solving problems at the University of Southern Mississippi for the Foundation of Post Secondary Education (FIPSE). As a sailor, Graham has crossed the Atlantic in a small sloop, sailed the Mediterranean and Aegean, and taught sailing there also. In addition, he holds the highest degree for celestial navigation (*Hochseeschifferzeugnis*) from Staatliche Hochschule feur Seefahrt, Lübeck. In 2000 Graham and his wife, Mary McKechnie-Graham, moved to Victoria, BC, Canada. He became President of the NDP provincial (Saanich South) and federal (Saanich-Gulf Islands) Constituencies, and was named an Honourary NDP Life Member. He wrote the current book of poetry (*The Inside World*) dedicated to the 50th anniversary of the death of his long-time friend and mentor, Wystan H. Auden, the foremost poet of the 20th century. He is now working on a book in philosophy, tentatively entitled "An Introduction to Person Theory."

Author and Dog, Alice

73

www.ingramcontent.com/pod-product-compliance
Lightning Source LLC
Chambersburg PA
CBHW071011120726
47910CB00004B/1472